W0009565

Hatfield Peverel
in old picture postcards volume 2

by Joyce P. Fitch

European Library ZALTBOMMEL/THE NETHERLANDS

Acknowledgements:

Mr. Nigel Bowdidge – information on Hatfield Peverel station.

Mr. Kenneth Frost – information on Hatfield Peverel station.

Mr. Ian Hook – Keeper of the Essex Regiment Museum.

Mr. Barry Finch – photographs of Fowler's ploughing engine.

Mr. C.P. Freeman – information on Fowler's ploughing engine.

Mr. Robert Pelly – information on the life of Mr. John Fowler.

Mrs. Helen Matcham – Hatfield Peverel map (permission for reproduction).

The National Motor Museum, Beaulieu.

Royal Historic Monuments Commission Essex (RHMCE) © Crown Copyright (permission for reproduction of photographs 55 and 66).

The Post Office Archives, Mount Pleasant.

The Essex Record Office, Chelmsford.

BACK IN TIME

GB ISBN 90 288 1147 8

© 1998 European Library – Zaltbommel/The Netherlands

Second edition, 1999: reprint of the original edition of 1998.

No part of this book may be reproduced in any form, by print, photoprint, microfilm or any other means, without written permission from the publisher.

Introduction

Why produce a second volume? The answer is simple – before it is too late. Not only do we still have pictures of how our village once looked but, equally importantly, we have the verbatim memories of some of the people who lived here when this century was young. A book of town pictures does not compare with that of a village; towns generate mostly photographs of shops and public buildings, but villages generate mainly those of homes and the people who lived in them.

The first volume created such interest and demand that I bought and sold the entire first print run of the first edition within a month, went straight into a second, and now, three years on, have only a couple of dozen left of the third. Because I was born in the village and believe in peopling the buildings pictured, I had the great pleasure of meeting up with older people (some of whom remembered me as a baby!), listening to their tales, then weaving them into a tapestry of Hatfield Peverel past. Thus it became a tangible memorial to their lives: the struggles when times were hard, the capers they got up to, and the fun of simple home-made entertainment. An added bonus was to meet many of those who bought the books, hear their reaction, and once again meet or correspond with villagers I had not seen for years. Newcomers to the village had the opportunity to see how life in Hatfield Peverel once was. An unforeseen bonus was that family historians from all over the world got in touch – not only could they read about the village and their ancestors, but they could see where they lived.

I find no reason to change the format for volume 2. Both the publisher and parishioners have asked for the book to be written and I have again received co-operation and encouragement from the local community and others living abroad. So many cards have emerged from lofts, suitcases, and all manner of hidey-holes, that again, not all can be included. The route I have followed through the village remains much the same, enabling me to fill in photographic gaps that had eluded me the first time round. I have also been able to extend the coverage of the parish – about seven square miles – by locating some hitherto unidentified places. For this I have to thank the owners for allowing me access to their properties.

Nounsley, which is not a separate village, was largely neglected in volume 1, as few cards came to light. This has been rectified. The adjoining parish of Ulting is so tiny that I decided to include some of its pictures and stories with its bigger neighbour – in ecclesiastical terms the two are twinned so it is nothing new. Covering an area of just over 1,000 acres, the population was never great. In 1881 it was 163; in 1917, 170; and in the last census of 1991 it was only 138, with Council tax returns of 1997 putting it at an estimated 154. Its nearest station was once at Langford on the LNER branch line from Witham to Maldon;

if Dr. Beeching could have seen into the future it would never have fallen foul of his axe. The village has one especial claim to fame: it was the home of the first beet sugar factory in the United Kingdom. This was operated in the early 1830s by Robert and James Marriage and a partner named Read, and in buildings situated not far from Hoe Mill. It did not exist for very long, but one of the flattened grassy spots on the Chelmer and Blackwater Navigation Canal is still known as *Sugar Bakers Hole*.

Occasionally I refer to photographs in this volume, and in volume 1. These entries appear as follows: card 5, volume 1, reads as (5V1) while card 3, in volume 2, reads as (3V2). Again I recommend the use of a magnifying glass where necessary. Because memories are so individual, it sometimes occurs that villagers of different names are recalled by several people as living at one address. Whenever possible I have tried to include at least some of the memories of people who actually inhabited the houses. Even then, succeeding generations can cause confusion. In our rural community few homes were owned; most were rented and often tied to the job. As villagers moved to find work – from farm to farm, and sometimes from one county to another – frequent mobility was often greater than today. I was interested to find that although some families had lived in the parish for years, several had moved into Essex from Suffolk.

Official, and most grateful, acknowledgements have been listed earlier. My thanks go to all who willingly loaned cards, told me their tales or who, in any way, helped me to put this book together. Joyce Dawson, Gwen Butler and Rosalie Kent were knowledgeable on the Baker family of Nounsley, while Reg Kent and Richard Rawlinson provided information on steam ploughs owned by that same family. In particular I would like to mention my good friends Gill and Alan Beach who came to my rescue with an identical word processor when my own gave up the ghost; the ever-patient, and skilled photographer Eric Morley who gave me so much of his time, and whose wife, Heather, allowed me to 'borrow' him; Mrs. Pamela Bowen-Davies for the gift of the reported local newscuttings of the 1920s and 1930s, written by her grandfather, Mr. Lindley Bott, and collected by her mother, Ruth. To produce even a slim volume takes a long time to research, and Mick, my husband, has uncomplainingly, lived for many months with piles of books and files littering the dining room table. Lastly, to you, my readers. May you, like me, learn something new about the two villages and find as much pleasure in the reading, as I have found in putting volume 2 together.

Joyce P. Fitch, Hatfield Peverel 1998

1 This map of the village was drawn by Miss Miriam Gepp in the late 1920s. It was the frontispiece of the book '*The Township of Hatfield Peverel*' (long out of print), written by her friend and near neighbour, Miss Teresa Hope of Crix. The charm and detail of the map warrants its inclusion and I am very grateful to Mrs. Helen Matcham, daughter of the late artist (10V2), for permission to reproduce it here. Apart from showing the area covered by Hatfield Peverel, Miss Gepp picked out and skilfully drew some of the most interesting features in the village which are now lost to us forever. Among these are Lungley's Cottage (otherwise known as Langley's), the Windmill and the old Workhouse. The age of the steam train has passed into oblivion and the farmworker hoeing by hand is rarely to be seen. Some names noted as early manors remain, including:

Smallands Farm, Termitts Farm, Mowden Hall, Bovingtons and Toppinghoe Hall.

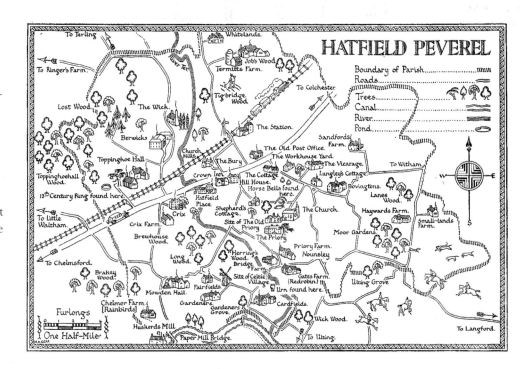

2 Ivy Cottage, the first house in the village beyond Boreham and quite unmistakable, stood at the entrance to the track (seen here) leading to Toppinghoe Hall. Ivy leaves obscure the sharp edges of the turreted roof but the Gothic-shaped lower window is quite distinct. Young Ruby Smith, whose father, Josiah, was a horseman for W. Seabrook & Sons, fruit growers, clutches her doll as she stands at the gate with her mother, Gertrude. A well in the front garden supplied fresh spring water and refreshed weary cyclists. On the back door hung a heavy chain where it is thought horses were tethered and rested by their owners riding on to London. Until it was blown down in a gale a wooden privy stood in the apple orchard behind the house; a replacement was made and delivered on a cart by Mr. Lewin, who positioned it in the yard. More convenient! Strange happenings in the house have been recalled by three different family occupants.

3   This aerial view of Toppinghoe Hall was taken before the bypass was built, the house being reached by the lane winding from Ivy Cottage on the old A12. Along this lane and over the hump-backed bridge crossing the railway came horses and carts to deliver goods: Oliver and Cleave, bread; Mr. Barker on Tuesday with wet fish; groceries from Witham Co-op. Top right grow rows of Seabrook's trees and in the grounds the fine old cedars, some still standing, can be clearly seen. The lower branches grew so flat that a cloth could be spread and a picnic laid. In 1925 William and Ivy Willis lived in the left half of the house while the Appletons lived next door. The Willis, Appleton and Smith families were all related. William had served with The Royal Horse Artillery and worked as horseman here (two were named Betsy and Major). Ivy was a maid at Crix. In a home where paraffin lamps and candles lit the darkness Aubrey and Bernard Willis were born.

4   Mr. and Mrs. Appleton lived in the nearer of the two cottages, once a much grander Hall. Alice Appleton is captured here standing among Seabrook's chickens and ducks that roamed freely round the yards. It has always been rumoured locally that an underground tunnel ran from Toppinghoe to New Hall in Boreham – built by Henry VIII for Anne Boleyn. What is *certain* is, that high up in the attic above Alice's head was hidden a little piece of village history. A young boy had stored some sweet chestnuts under the floorboards there, the mice had found them and in his search for these thieves the boy made some exciting discoveries. Hidden from view were: a dagger, a leather pouch, and fragments of cloth armour, all dating from the 1600s. The cloth armour still exists and in recent times was bought by a Mr. Townsend; a family of this name once lived at Berwick Place and at Crix. A drawing of the armour can be seen at Colchester Library.

5   Back to the main road and a rear view of Crix. Extensive grounds, once tended by six gardeners, slope away to the south. Mr. Mick Crane spent around 63 years of his life as gardener here. A startling and inexplicable event, possibly linked to Crix, has recently come to light. On 13th September 1980, Mr. and Mrs. Peter Mickelsen were driving along the Terling road approaching Crix. Suddenly, a large black and white animal, the size of a small cow, came hurtling down the left bank, hit the car with a thud, went underneath and let out a long, sickening scream. Fearful of what they might find they took a torch to investigate. There was nothing to be seen – no animal remains, no blood, no damage to the car. On arrival home they phoned people in the location without success and reported the incident to Witham police station. Some years later Peter read of the eerie story of Shaen's Shaggy Dog, as told in the first volume (1V1).

CRIX, HATFIELD PEVEREL

6 How many pairs of feet once sauntered along this peaceful path lying beside the River Ter? Winter sun shines on bare branches of trees and bushes and highlights the wooden palings of the fence; the gentle rippling of the water soothes our minds as it flows out of sight beside us on the right. The gate invites us to lift the latch and venture further. Beyond the Viaducts a footpath on the left takes us across the field to Wick Farm. Even the tumbledown shed speaks to us of time to spare. The solitude is only occasionally broken as a steam train rattles importantly across the Viaduct, built especially to carry the track over the Ter valley. Before railways sig-nalled places of danger, Springtime would find these banks dotted with small groups of children gathering bunches of deep blue or white violets, both sweetly-scented. Wrapped in their heart-shaped leaves they were lovingly tied with a length of wool or cotton.

HATFIELD PEVEREL. 1790.

7   It was along this Terling Hall road that Peter and Mandy Mickelsen were returning (5V2). We are facing the opposite direction, have passed Berwick Place and approach Wick Farm on the right, where, at a leisurely pace, a driver guides the horse round yet another curve in the narrow lane. Country lanes usually evolved from the perimeters of field patterns, rambling round edges which were marked out centuries before. Wick Farm itself is old, dating from the 1600s, its two original chimney stacks having eight-sided shafts. It was close to here, and tantalisingly just out of sight on the left, that one of the several village brickfields lay. The scene seems quiet but the summer months saw the men hard at work: digging out the pug; hand-moulding the bricks; firing them in the kiln and stacking them by the thousand on racks. Former workers at the brickfields reckon the bricks from Nounsley were the most highly rated for quality.

8   Leafless trees, starkly etched against a Winter sky, are mirrored in the still waters of the Ter. At this point the water we see is in a cut, dug out to take the river in time of flood. We have a clear view of the Mill House with the imposing structure of the Mill itself beyond. To our left an island was created on which stood a summer-house. The whole area was loved by villagers, but the waters also served a more practical purpose. Water from the river replenished the boilers of traction engines, ploughing machines, threshing tackle, fairground engines and Council water carts. In Summer, Council carts sprinkled water on to rough roads thick with dust. The body of the cart was like a big tank on wheels with shafts on the sides. A hose was put into the water and pumped by hand to fill the tank which was then pulled (up the steep hill!) by two horses. Others who drove horses and carts would come with pails to give drink to the thirsty animals.

THE MILL

HATFiELD PEVEREL, NEAR CHELMSFORD.   107

9 The Mill House, built in 1715, is seen here dwarfed by the Mill itself. Standing five storeys high, with a pitched gable roof, it was built of 17th-century bricks; all the original woodwork was deal. Opposite the house a rustic bridge with white railings spanned the cut in the river, giving access to the island with its hexagonal-shaped summer house. Below the bridge was an old trap and it is said that on one night alone 7½ hundredweights of eels were caught. When Colonel Arkwright owned the Mill, thinking to add another touch of wildlife to this stretch of water, he planted a few bull-rushes. These rapidly spread and can be seen encroaching to the left of the picture. The photographer has positioned a central, solitary figure: a strange place in which to stand, for it is enveloped by the long shadow cast by a tree on the opposite side of the road. The rough-edged pavement leads the eye up the hill to the village.

The Mill, Hatfield Peverel.

10 This is a special wedding photograph. The happy couple, caught by the camera, pose in the front garden of Hill House, opposite the entrance to Bury Lane in the Street. The trellis-topped and rose-sprayed brick wall still stand. The date is 11th June 1929, the groom is Mr. Lionel Harrison, while the fetching bride is Miriam Gepp, creator of the map we saw earlier. The sun shines warmly as a light breeze stirs the hems of the bridesmaids' dresses. Hill House was the Gepp family home, and Mr. Thomas Gepp, brother of the bride, recalls happy times spent here. Among many things, he remembers how in the days before household refrigeration, cartloads of ice from H. Cutts, Witham fishmonger and ice merchant, would be shot into the deep cellars beneath the house. The groom too is part of our story, for it was his father, the Rev. H.G. Harrison, who in 1920 revived the custom of 'Beating the Bounds' – marking out the perimeter of the parish.

11 Another group. Despite the sombre faces a good time was about to be had by all! Few early photographs of the interior of the old village hall (15V1), such as this, have withstood much handling over the years. Each year the Noble Order of Buffaloes laid on a spread for the elderly, and it is, no doubt, the photographer's command to 'Hold It!' that accounts for the somewhat grim expressions on most faces. The entrance to the hall from the Street lies to the left of the standing figure, with the double-doored emergency exit at the back. Many villagers wondered what would have happened in this well-used room in the event of fire, for it was often crowded to capacity – and several more squeezed in after that! On this occasion, at least, all was well and seconds after the photographer had recorded the event, faces would have broken into smiles, the air would have been filled with the babble of voices, the jingling of cutlery and clinking of glasses.

12   Cigarette drooping from his bottom lip, young James Lawrence poses nonchalantly outside this grocery shop in the Street. Research reveals that the vehicle is an Overland (PU1334) and was registered on 1st January 1924 in the name of Mr. J. Lawrence, The Stores, Hatfield Peverel. This came as a surprise to his grandson, Mr. Ken Lawrence, for he had believed it to come from one of the larger residences, who sometimes collected their orders. The shop, which sold all manner of goods beside groceries, stayed open until 10 p.m. and Ken recalls that one particular customer regularly came in on a Saturday to buy the weekly shopping – exactly three minutes before closing time! As a lad he slept in one of the bedrooms and remembers hearing the rats from the adjoining Forge scurrying across the attic floor above. The Methodist Chapel stands on the left, much the same today, while the tree gives its name to Fir Tree Cottages set back from the road.

13 On a wintry photographic excursion, Fred Spalding must have stumbled on this historic gathering outside the Swan public house. Enlargement shows and research reveals that the faded sign over the door reads 'Russell's Gravesend Brewery Ltd', a name used by the Writtle Brewery Company which ceased brewing in 1907. Where 'teas and light refreshments' were once served in the garden, a terrace of five houses have this year (1998) been built and the right-hand bay window has been demolished. The photograph is of the Bedfordshire Yeomanry (probably the 1/1st) who were stationed in the village from August 1914 until June 1915. On their right breasts they display the Imperial Service badge (which became obsolete around 1915) denoting that they had agreed to serve outside the UK if required. The Bandolier worn across the chest contained 15 rounds of .303 ammunition. How many, one wonders, of these smiling faces were to return to Britain's shores?

14 This formal photograph shows one soldier, at least, who did return. He is Trooper Douglas Robinson of D Squadron, a sergeant in the Bedfordshire Yeomanry. During times of war, relationships, some lasting, were formed with local girls. This particular girl is Rose Twin, who met Douglas when he was stationed here and she was working as a maid. They fell in love, and here, Rose, prettily dressed, gloved, and with a stylish hat upon her head, takes her sweetheart's arm to stand before the camera. He went off to fight in France, survived having his horse shot from beneath him and in 1918 he and Rose were married. Whether this photograph was taken before or at their wedding is unclear, but it carries on the facing side of the card the inscription 'There's gladness in remembrance'. In our churchyard one of the same regiment lies buried: he is 1112 Private T. Adamson, who died on 1st January 1915. Two endings: one happy, one sad.

15   Old ways begin to give way to new. Here, on the corner of Station Road and the Street, a petrol station has been erected to serve the slowly increasing number of people driving motorised vehicles. The distinctive signs of B.P. and *Shell* stand out on the forecourt. It was owned by Albert Cable and his wife Bessie, daughter of Horace Moore. New homes have begun to spring up in the once empty space beyond Quince Cottage and we can just see the blank wall of a new business: that of Percy Cresswell's drug store, where he sold medication for all kinds of ailments. Quite unconcerned, a pony munches the hedge on the right, which at this time bordered the field given by Mr. N. de Bond as a recreation field to the village. A two-wheeled light cart slewed across the road indicates the lack of traffic. The signpost leads into Post Office path (now Bennett Way), the Post Office itself then occupying today's site of Barclays Bank.

16 The much-needed and long-awaited Hatfield Peverel bypass was eventually built, but not without heartache for some. Most, if not all, of the homes seen here on the left were demolished to make way for its passage. In all, fifteen dwellings disappeared, including that of Mr. R. Sorrell the butcher, and the one owned by Mrs. V. Cullen (74V2), who moved here from Ulting after the death of her husband. Their houses stood on the right. Marina Road was cut short. Most of the area we see here now forms part of the fly-over bridge in Station Road, one of three needed to allow traffic to flow freely on the dual carriageway deep in the gully below. It was opened in 1965 when Mr. Ernest Marples was Minister for Transport. He will be remembered by many for his habitual riding of a bicycle and the wearing of cycle clips. No doubt, however, as befitted the occasion, dignitaries at the opening ceremony arrived at Hatfield Peverel in style – by motor car.

Station Road, Hatfield Peverel.

17 This neat, terraced row of cottages, is situated in the lane that leads to the station yard. In the gap that lies between them and the building on the right (Temperance Hotel and Yew Tree Cottage), is the modern estate of The Pines. As a child Emma Pease lived in a cottage nearer the station and some of her memories are worth recollection. She had two elder brothers and writes: … *but being a mere girl I was not allowed to ride the miniature penny-farthing bicycle they owned, that being a business proposition as well as pleasure, the charge being ¹/₂d a ride to all-comers.* She remembers: *the old gentleman leaning on the wall surrounding his garden smoking his churchwarden pipe, the old lady that mangled the weekly wash at 2¹/₂d a day in an old-fashioned box-mangle containing stones, and the rat-catcher in his cart with cream-coloured pony, and a box of ferrets in the back. His wife wore a black lace cap and mittens. The couple lived in Yew Tree Cottage.*

HATFIELD PEVEREL. 24.

18 This Spalding view, seen from the London-bound platform, complements two of 1915 depicted in (23, 24, V1). The covered wooden footbridge can be seen and the manually controlled signals, beyond which, on the left, we glimpse a waggon near one of the sidings which bordered the vast goods yard. It is now a car park, for goods facilities ceased on 27th June 1960. In the foreground on the right the gent's urinal (with water tank on top) carries advertisements and we have a clear view of the old shelter. The first station was probably a simple wooden structure and listed only as 'Hatfield'; a timetable exists for 1845 listing times and prices between Liverpool Street Station and Colchester. The fire which totally destroyed our station was reported in the *Essex County Standard* on 23rd February 1849. It was not rebuilt until 1878, which explains the mysterious lack of a mention in Trade Directories between the two dates. Trains merely 'passed through'.

G.E. RAILWAY STATION, HATFIELD PEVEREL 1855

19 There has been a dwelling at Termitts since ancient times, and this photograph shows the front of the present house which dates from the early 1500s. Two upper storeys are clearly shown projecting at the end of the cross-wings. In his 1920 account of 'Beating the Bounds' the Rev. Harrison, then vicar here, states: ... *A section of the circuit was taken on each of the three Rogation Days, May 10th, 11th, 12th. On May 10th we assembled at Whitelands where Hon. E.G. Strutt kindly entertained us to tea; both churchwardens were present, and there was a considerable following, including young people and budding scouts (duly equipped with the proper willow wand). Our route lay NE. along the Terling roadside, round by Pitfields Barns, generally known as Dancing Dicks, doubling back almost to Termitt's and then round to Job's Wood.* Locations named in this age-old custom of thus marking the parish boundaries can be found on Miriam Gepp's map.

20   From halfway to Terling we return to an aerial view of the Street before the village was bypassed. Where we see cut swathes of stubble, now, parallel to the old A12, runs a double swathe of roads. Fronting the road in the right-hand corner stands Mr. Claydon's garage business with a separate petrol station adjoining. The houses, although modernised to become 'Hooks and Sheaves' and 'Salvadore', still stand. On the opposite side of the road may be seen the shop begun by Mr. Wood, greengrocer, its shade pulled down to protect the fruit and vegetables. Next door lie various buildings culminating at the far right in the Duke of Wellington pub and its outbuildings. A faint but interesting line runs diagonally from right to left in the bottom left-hand corner. This was a long footpath, one of several lost to the village, which led from the Street across the fields to the railway station. Today it would pass through the flats of Priory Court.

21 Field sports were once considered a normal part of rural life, and this Meet at the Duke of Wellington pub was nothing out of the ordinary. The photograph is dated 1904. That there would ever be room on the forecourt for all the horses and hounds, today seems quite extraordinary. In Miriam Gepp's map the fox may be detected making good his escape into woodland near Moor Gardens; other sports abounded too, for hare-coursing and otter hunting are reported in local newspapers. Pheasants proliferated and at a shoot at Crix of eight guns, 402 birds were bagged. Before motorised transport became the norm, the road was often empty of traffic – so empty in fact that a newspaper of around 1900 carries an interesting report. It tells (in kindly terms) of a workman from Toppinghoe Hall, who having enjoyed his evening drinking, lay down in the road outside the pub and went to sleep! Unfortunately, 'the poor chap' was run over by the mail coach.

Meet at Duke of Wellington Hatfield Peverel.

H. Hall. Photo. Witham.

22   Few vehicles would take issue with this magnificent machine as it edges its way on to the old A12 opposite the Terrace and turns towards the village. It is a Fowler ploughing engine named *Dreadnought* and Ted Rawlinson, owner and driver, pauses to allow passage to an early AA patrol motorbike with side car to pass. Ted has been pulling out fruit trees from Mr. Wadley's orchard. His machine is a Class BB compound cylinder 14 NHP (nominal horse power), its engine number is 14222 and its registration number is NK 1963. Manufactured in 1914 it began its working life in Hertfordshire. At some time later it was bought by Baker Bros. of Nounsley and so to Ted Rawlinson. Ted himself came from a farming background and married Ella, daughter of Ernest Baker. Ploughing engines were built in pairs – a right-hand machine and a left-hand machine. *Dreadnought's* other half: 14221 NK 1962, since scrapped, was called *Lord Roberts*.

23 With grey smoke puffing from its chimney, *Dreadnought* has ground slowly and noisily on past the Wayside Café (still open for business near Hatfield Heights estate) and is now opposite the Wellington pub. When Mr. Finch took this photograph he could not have known that the massive Greyhound Barn would one day no longer exist. Mr. John Upson recalls that Council engines were kept in the yard between the Barn and Tudor Lodge, the building on the right. When machines being prepared for use were getting up steam, they were so noisy that some of the nearby residents became 'steamed up' as well! Tudor Lodge has stood for around five hundred years and was probably once much larger. An official report written in 1975 reads: *The above property appears to date from circa 1500. It is either the cross-wing to a larger house, since demolished, or a smaller house similar in accommodation to the Chantry Priests House in Maldon*...

24 We stand opposite the Wellington pub in the front garden of Mr. and Mrs. Fred Brett. Facing us is the blank end wall of No. 3 Chestnut Cottages, while the ornamental iron arch wrought by Henry Harris and William spans the entrance to Blacksmith's Yard. The occasion is a solemn one: the dedication of the British Legion Standard. A local paper records the event and we can identify some of the participants. Kneeling is Mr. Oliver Old, standard bearer, supported by Mr. Frank Watson and Mr. Victor Prior. The procession had paraded from Hill House (10V2), the residence of Mr. Hamilton Gepp (Under-Sheriff of Essex), and was attended by Legion members from Chelmsford, Maldon, Woodham Walter and Danbury. The local Salvation Army Band was joined by that of the Maldon and Langford corps. At this moment of presentation onlookers have removed their caps as Colonel Eustace Hill, D.S.O. (Master of the East Essex Foxhounds) completes the ceremony.

25 A rough track leading from the Street, under Henry Harris's archway, takes us into Blacksmith's Yard. Here, once stood five cottages: a block of three and another of two. Regularly as clockwork the Salvation Army Band played here each Sunday evening at 6 p.m. The smiling face of Bill Willis greets us in his front garden and his granddaughter, Ruby Eggleton, remembers him as being full of fun. The houses had long back gardens where vegetables were grown while flowers filled the front gardens. Other names recalled as living here are Mrs. Dennis, Clara Bell (a great knitter of socks for her daughter, Jessie), and William and Sarah Wright. The Wrights had a codling apple tree in the garden while their neighbours, the Digbys, had bullace trees. They also had a well. Mr. Digby walked with two sticks and on beginning his long trek to the privy at the bottom of the garden would announce 'I'm just going to visit Boreham!' (a village adjacent).

26   The Salvation Army was established in the village over a century ago. Its first meetings appear to have been held in the upper part of what is now a dentist's surgery in the Street. They then met in an old cottage on the Green, but the site that will be remembered by many villagers will be the one seen here in Maldon Road, where a bungalow called The Hollies now stands. A newspaper announcement made on 9th June 1920 revoked the earlier certificate granting a place of worship, dated 4th May 1904. The photograph shows the newer premises and was taken from the gateway of Holly House (once Harold Lawrence's shop). On Sundays, and some weekdays, the wooden walls reverberated to the lusty sound of hymn singing, and music played by the brass band and timbrels. The lorry, advertising the good sense of keeping Bovril in the emergency store cupboard, suggests the early 1940s. A small arm belonging to one of the Lawrence family reaches out of the pram.

27 These photographs of the front of Langford Cottages were taken by the owner, the late Mr. May, before and after restoration. They are included because some readers of volume I found it difficult to believe they are the same property. In a well-informed book written about agriculture Mr. May states: *All the original oak timbering was uncovered and more old oak added to match.* From Mount Pleasant Post Office Headquarters in London I unearthed the following: 26th October 1843. *As the number of letters for the villages of Springfield, Boreham and Hatfield Peverell near Chelmsford, account to upwards of 500 in a week, I submit an official Post office be established at the expense of 14s a week to include delivery of the letters by a foot Messenger and £4. per annum each for the Receivers at Springfield, Boreham and Hatfield Peverell.* The first Post Master or Receiver was Charles Todd and the office was in the room behind the bow window.

28 Toulmin Road branches off from New Road and was built in the form of a cul-de-sac in the early 1930s. The then modern-looking houses had no sewerage but each was served by a brick-built privy at the rear of the building. With no electricity, winter nights meant a foray into the dark. There was no piped water. With pails in hand, the inhabitants fetched the water (several times a day – especially for Monday clothes washing) from a pump in what was known as 'The Ring' at the top of the road and nearest the camera. A concrete path leading to the hand pump can just be seen between the grass verges at the bottom of the picture. The road was named after the Rev. F.B. Toulmin, vicar of the parish from 1874 to 1917. At some time before his ordination he was almost drowned at sea and vowed, that should he survive, he would take Holy Orders. Although he was a somewhat unconventional vicar he gained the respect and affection of his parochial flock.

29 *Dreadnought* has passed the end of New Road to arrive in front of the six, terraced, brick-built, Vicarage Cottages. Many a boot and shoe was 'soled and heeled' by Mr. W. Hume, in the shed behind his home here, now part of Woodham Drive Estate. By a quirk of fate, John Fowler, *Dreadnought's* creator, has associations with the village. It was Fowler, who, at the time when steam power was making its presence felt by way of steam travel, became convinced that the same power could be used in agriculture. After years of dedication and experimentation he achieved his goal in 1858. Against much competition he was awarded the Gold Medal and £500 offered by the Royal Agricultural Society for Steam Ploughing. In 1864, his health suffered because of overwork, and whilst out horseriding, he fell, contracted anthrax, and died. He was just 38. One of his descendants, Canon Pelly, was associated with our church, and great-great-granddaughter, Mrs. O. Nelmes, still lives here.

30 The Parish Magazine for 1908 carries this advertisement: *Miss Courtman, Dressmaker, Salisbury Cottage.* This is the house on the far right where one-armed Mr. Courtman kept a shop selling sweets, wool, buttons and home-cured bacon. Aniseed balls were 20 for 1d. One of his daughters was a skilled needlewoman making many a bride's wedding dress. At this time the Barker family lived next door. Later, the Miller family lived at Salisbury Cottage and son Bob recalls that, at the rear of the house his father had a smallholding of around three quarters of an acre. He grew blackcurrant bushes, potatoes and peas, and kept pigs and chickens.

Bob remembers that the two trees proved an exciting place for him and his brothers to climb. Behind the seven cottages pictured here ran a private footpath. It started next to the Parish Room (out of sight on the left) and led to the communal privy which stood on Miller land. The little boy is Bill Chapman.

31 At the age of 92, Mrs. Fanny Mynett, a widow, died at No. 2 of the four Lovibond Almshouses in Maldon Road. She bore thirteen children, nine of whom at one time were seriously ill with typhoid fever; one died. In 1925, while a young lad at the neighbouring school, grandson Ernie Barker, regularly called in to have his dinner. His mother worked at the Vicarage which was then next door. Residents, in accordance with the Will of Martha Lovibond who founded the dwellings, also received ten shillings a week. The State Pension (instituted in 1908) brought in another ten shillings, and Ernie recalls that occasionally she was able to purchase a pheasant (costing half-a-crown) from the Sainsbury's van which delivered to the door. The room on the right was the living room, the one on the left the bedroom. Cooking was done on a coal range and a paraffin stove, while water came from a communal pump. The pretty little porch still has a seat on either side.

32 Through the central wrought-iron gate many pairs of feet went willingly, or unwillingly, into school. Railings on either side stretched as far as the two stalwart brick pillars; now only the railings on the right give evidence that the building ever existed. Ivy clings to the front wall of the headmaster's house and climbing roses overshadow part of his downstairs window. Known probably only to few, two bricks, screened behind the roses, formed a bench-mark which on the Ordnance Survey map denoted the school's height above sea-level. Wooden palings completed the length of either playground, both of which once echoed to the high-pitched shrieks of children enjoying a respite from lessons. Just inside the gate is a flagpole. On Empire Day (24th May) Brownies, Wolf Cubs, Girl Guides and Boy Scouts would don their uniforms, and, to lusty singing of the National Anthem by the whole school, saluted as the Union Jack was raised.

33   Here, in a Chrismas card setting, the church and churchyard lie blanketed in snow. A photograph and information on the building were given in volume I (54V1), but the scene merits inclusion here if only to tell a tale. Christmas 1897 was not a happy time for the village, for a newscutting of December 24th reads: *For some time past the influenza has been prevalent in Hatfield Peverel, and towards the end of last week, Mr. W. Havis, the carrier to Witham, was laid up and unable to find a substitute for two or three days. The church organist and most of the choir ... were in the same plight, and speculation was rife as to how the services at the Church on Sunday would be got through without them, when at the eleventh hour the matter* *was decided in an unexpected way. The Vicar (the Rev. F.B. Toulmin) was taken ill and unable to leave his room. There was no time to arrange 'a supply' and the services at the Parish Church could not be held.*

34 This front view of the Priory, built in 1768 for John Wright, a London coach-maker, was not as he would have seen it at that time. Victorian hands added the ugly porch and downpipes, destroying the simplicity of its outlines – outlines which its present owners sought to, and have succeeded in, restoring. During this period of hard work a gilt button bearing the Wright family crest was found under floorboards. The Priory will be remembered by villagers as the home of the Tennant family before becoming headquarters of the Marianhill Religious Mission. During the Second World War it rang, as never before, to the sound of children's voices, for it became a school. Many pupils and staff of the Trinity County Grammar School, Wood Green, filled its rooms for lessons and were billeted throughout the village. It says much for their affection for Hatfield Peverel that, more than fifty years on, many still return to recapture memories and meet up with old friends.

35   The opportunity to show a different view of Shepherd's Cottage was one too good to miss. For hundreds of years it was the only house standing between the Street corner and the entrance to the church. The wealth of trees is striking; so many of them have now been cut down. In a Directory of 1864 it is stated that of the 4,929 acres, 2 roods and 28 perches comprising Hatfield Peverel (close on 5,000 acres), one tenth – 508 acres – were woodland. Shepherd's Cottage in its unrestored state has been home to many large families, the Collars, Wagstaffs and Does to name but three. Opposite the cottage was a spring-fed ram (a hydraulic water-raising device) and it was the task of Annie and Mercy Doe to drop empty pails beside it on the way to school and fill them up at dinner time. This they repeated in the afternoon. On wash-days their three brothers took over the task for many brimming pails were needed for the copper in which clothes were boiled.

36 Mr. Edwards ran a small dairy at Crabbs Farm. He had about eight cows, mainly Jersey, and his son, Frank, and daughter, Kitty, hand-milked the cows; milk was bottled on the premises. He also owned a horse and a pony. At six o'clock each morning Mr. Kenneth Rayner arrived for work to deliver the milk. To catch the pony was not always easy, but as where the horse went the pony invariably followed, he used to chase the horse into a deep ditch, jump on to its back, then grab the pony and harness it to a small cart. His round, on which he delivered milk, cream and eggs, took him along the Street to Crix, following the by-road to Brakeys then down the hill via the ford to Nounsley. Mr. Edwards also manufactured cream ices. At Crabbs Lodge, opposite, lived the Davey family and George recalls his brother, Jack, pedalling a trade bike round the village at weekends selling the ice cream which was kept frozen on a trolley of dry ice.

CRABBES FARM, HATFIELD PEVEREL

37   Crabbs House, the back of which (seen here) overlooks the Ter valley, has views of rural beauty to the south which take in the slopes of Little Baddow. Standing in grounds opposite Crabbs Farm it is now a nursing home. In the early 1900s it was owned by Mr. and Mrs. Bramwell, the latter a professional soprano singer and sister of Clara Butt. Mrs. Bramwell involved herself musically in the village by putting on concerts, bringing well-known artists to the house for performances, and, in conjunction with Mr. A. Bennett, headmaster, by promoting music and singing at the village school. At a time when Hatfield Peverel had four bands, the Choral Society, also under the tuition of the Bramwells, achieved many successes in County championships. Later occupiers were to be the Kaye family, who lived here from 1917 to 1938; the Master of Kinnaird and his family, and more recently, Mike Reid, television and stage actor.

38   Further down Crabbs Hill we take the sharp turning on the left into Sportsman's Lane. Here, the thatched cottage (then two homes) can be clearly seen; today, tall hedgerows obscure this view. Its name, Gregorys, probably dates from a previous owner, a Lieutenant Gregory. During roof renovation workmen found the skeleton of a cat in the attic, an old superstition for warding off evil. Taking no chances, the present owner instructed that it should remain. The copse at the rear of the house is given an intriguing mention in the deeds, namely: it must never be felled. Local folklore believes it is the graveyard of nuns. Could they have been from the earlier Benedictine Priory just a stone's throw across the fields? The copse shelters owls, pigeons, magpies, foxes, squirrels, pheasants, rats, mice, and bats – which have been known to come down the chimney! During the Second World War, on today's garage site, a searchlight probed the dark skies.

GREGORIES, HATFIELD PEVEREL

39   This attractive walk will be found by following the signpost next to Gregorys. Sloping down to the River Ter we come to a narrow, wooden-planked bridge flanked by outward leaning metal rails. At this point the waters are very shallow and fishing was a favourite childhood pastime; gudgeon, loach and sticklebacks, caught with a homemade net, were transported home in a glass jam jar with string tied around the neck to incorporate a handle. A picnic always accompanied such an expedition and was usually consumed on arrival – wrist watches were beyond the reach of most families' pockets. In any case the eating was as much part of the pleasure as the fishing. Always in view was the windmill. For children living in that area their regular route to school lay along a footpath opposite Gardener's Cottage, which skirted Herrings Wood. No trace of the wood remains and the windmill (76V1) was pulled down in 1942.

FOOTPATH TO WINDMILL, HATFIELD PEVEREL

40   Back to Maldon Road and a house that stood close to the Wheatsheaf pub. On the map it is called Lungley's Cottage, but old records refer to it as 'Langley's'. James Lungley, village carpenter and parish clerk, once lived here, which possibly accounts for the confusion. At another time it was occupied by the Ketley family who let two rooms to a Mrs. Hale and it is mentioned in (62V1) as having a draughty keyhole which provided a cure for a sty on the eye! This particular card comes with an inscription on the back when it was the home of the Poulton family. Dated 2nd October 1914 and addressed to Mr. Brinley Poulton it reads: *Wishing you many Happy Returns, from your ever loving mother.* Brinley was the second of the six sons and four daughters of Ellen and William Poulton, head brewer of Brown's Brewery. The flag of St. George flies from the pole behind the chimney stack – probably an act of patriotism as the First World War had just begun.

41 When the Co-operative Society acquired Langley's it was demolished and a new store built on the site. In 1917 the Society is reported as taking £24 a week; by 1931 it had risen to £100. Certainly the store was an important part of village life at the time and with its big bay-fronted windows, it was the last word in modernity. Consumables are artistically stacked in the left window and hard goods on the right. An even earlier picture shows materials, elegantly draped, occupying this second side. A newscutting reads: *The new building is replete with every convenience, and living accommodation is provided for the manager on the first floor.* On the steps with his staff is a later manager, Mr. Arthur Britton. For many years now, and named Peverel House, the building has been an office block. In January of this year (1998) the bays were removed to reveal red bricks bearing the stamp of 'Marriage' from the Nounsley brickyard.

42　A few doors on from the Co-op and dressed in early uniform – the women with long skirts and all with assorted hats – stands the Salvation Army Band. Above the low doorway of this cottage (since demolished and now called Greenaways) the name of the organisation is proudly displayed. It appears in a wider context in volume 1 (65V1) and was once the home of three families. Some of the soldiers here are known by name: far left, Bill Pease; next, Mr. Gibson, senior, who walked the four miles from Rivenhall and at lunchtime went to eat with the drummer who lived opposite.

Harry White (owner of the house and small tin-roofed shop on the Green) is third, while a member of the Wright family towers over minute Tommy Spearman, shoe-mender, supporting the big drum he banged. Bill's wife, Emma, is seated and holding a squeeze-box. A pleasingly rural touch in our picture is the sight of a large cabbage growing in the bottom left-hand corner.

43   Sturdy horses were once used for haulage purposes on the local farms. These four splendid animals, seen with horsemen, Mr. Wilks and Mr. Langstone, worked on Bovingtons Farm in Maldon Road. A stack of hay made in the traditional shape stands behind. From horses comes manure, much prized by villagers in the cultivation of their vegetable patches, and, if deposited in the road it comes free of charge! A news report of 3rd April 1900 tells of: ... *an old inhabitant of Hatfield Peverel, named William Rawlinson, aged 70, while stooping in the road opposite the Post Office, gathering manure, was knocked down by a pony driven by a lad named Bertie Bickmore, in the employ of Mr. C. Moore,* baker ... *Horace Moore, then aged 17, witnessed the accident. He said ... A four-wheeler belonging to his father came round the station corner at a slow pace.* The verdict was Accidental Death. In 1900 the Post Office was between Heylis florist shop and the Tyre Centre.

44 Detective work was required to locate this, and the following photograph. By picking out individual letters on the round woven baskets the name of 'Morse' can be deciphered and a newscutting of 1890 pinpoints the orchard as Barnards Farm, close to the village boundary with Wickham Bishops. Mr. Percy Morse who began to plant at Michaelmas 1885, had, by 1890, fifty acres under fruit cultivation. He employed: … *150 to 250 local women and children together with others from Witham, Langford, Ulting and Rivenhall.* The men gathered up the baskets for despatch to market; the farm still has boxes marked 'Morse'. At the end of the fruit harvest the big barn (still standing) was cleared for a celebration when … *About 150 sat down to tea, the Salvation Army band played, Mr. Payne of Chipping Hill read 'The Jackdaw of Rheims' and Mr. Morse was presented with a handsome engraved inkstand.* From 250 acres of orchards in 1938, none now remain.

45 At Barnards Farm, where the present owner remembers the two distinctive post uprights, another crop was potatoes. Notice the close resemblance of the only man, to the one standing far right in the previous picture: he was undoubtedly the 'gaffer'. Here he has donned a jacket as he works with the women to bag potatoes from the straw-covered clamp made the previous year. A sharp frost can turn potatoes black and render them rotten so insulation was essential. About this period women wore broad-brimmed hats – even to work in the fields. In 1938 potatoes formed the highest percentage of crops with almost 1,100 acres under cultivation; potato-picking is still a back-aching job, usually carried out by women. A horse-drawn plough digs deep into the earth, uprooting and turning over the plants to bring the tubers to the surface. The women gather them in pails, empty them into sacks, and the smell of newly-turned soil fills the nostrils.

46 So well known in the village was Sydney Letch, that the corner on which he lived on the Maldon Road near Ulting, became known as Letch's Corner. When both were 16 Sydney met his future bride, Elizabeth. They married five years on, in 1917, but he could not see her in her wedding finery, for by then, Sydney was blind. Shot by a sniper's bullet in the First World War, he was trained at St. Dunstan's as a mat-maker, an occupation at which he excelled. Local people bought his mats – and so did the Queen and the Queen Mother. His workshop can be seen behind them here, where they lean on the gate with their son John.

Elizabeth helped with another successful venture: poultry keeping and the rearing of pigs. A strong-minded woman, she, like her husband, was not lacking in courage. Early in their marriage of 64 years, they travelled by tandem, drove a pony and trap, while at one time Elizabeth transported them both in a motor cycle combination.

47   Back to the Green. This glass, brimming with 'the crystal ale' was the trade mark of Edwin Rust & Co., Brewers, Maltsters, Spirit and Cigar Merchants. In *Durrant's Handbook for Essex* of 1887 it reads: *Established over 40 Years*. Mr. Rust, listed in a trade directory of 1859, later lived at Peverel Cottage, and the Brewery functioned for a further thirty-nine years. It was reopened by a Mr. Charles Brown. Giving evidence on 9th June 1898 at a meeting of the Beer Materials Committee, Mr. Brown stated: … *The Brewery was shut up and everything sold off some six months ago. I started brewing from English malt and hops only … I exhibit a label on every cask that goes out … and we have a small label for the bottle … Trade increases every year and I am doing about 2,000 barrels a year … The Brewery is pictured in volume 1 (66V1).* Comparing prices of yester-year, when wages would have been but a fraction of those today, holds a certain fascination.

Established over 40 Years.
HATFIELD PEVEREL BREWERY.
E. RUST & Co.,
BREWERS, MALTSTERS, SPIRIT, & CIGAR
MERCHANTS.

£1 1s. per   10s. 6d. per
18   9
GALLONS.   GALLONS.

THE CRYSTAL ALE

TRADE MARK.

PRICE LIST.

	Per Gal.	Per Bar.		Per Gal.	Per Bar.
XXXX OLD ..	2/-	72/-	XXX PALE ALE	1/4	48/-
XXX½ OLD ..	1/6	54/-	XX PALE ALE	1/-	36/-
XXX ..	1/2	42/-	STOUT, Double	1/6	54/-
XX MILD ..	1/-	36/-	„ Single	1/4	48/-
X	-/10	30/-	PORTER.. ..	1/-	36/-

2s. *per Barrel*, **1s.** *per Kilderkin*, **6d.** *per Firkin*, and **2d.** *per dozen Bottles allowed as Discount for Cash on Delivery.*

Spirit List sent Post Free on Application.

48 This is almost the southern tip of the Green. It is hard to imagine how it must have looked when it once stretched from here to the old Roman Road. The butcher's shop roof has been heightened, the little general shop still thrives and fairly early examples of both car and bus have arrived. Mr. H. White has departed, and the shop is here being run by Mrs. Madeleine Sorrell, selling the usual miscellany of goods including groceries, confectionery, and hanks or balls of wool. Her husband, Vivian, bought the bus from Harold Stracey who first started a public service in 1922. Muriel Wood remembers having a lift up Hatfield Hill – steep by local standards – to get to school. It was for school-runs, too, that Viv Sorrell often operated, especially after older children transferred for secondary education at Witham in 1937. James Wilkinson senior, manager of Hatfield Wick brickworks, was another early bus proprietor. See (7, 50V2).

49 All the way from Australia this photograph has come home to rest. It is of old weather boarded houses on the Green glimpsed distantly in volume 1 (70V1). Frederick Atkinson, seen here in his trap, with Colonel, the dog, seated alongside, was baptised in 1862. He married Emily Butcher of Castle Hedingham in 1882, and she can be seen in the doorway above which the sign reads *F. Atkins, Chimney Sweep*. Of their eleven children six emigrated to Canada. The little lad, Fred, here aged four, was born in 1902, dating the scene to 1906, and it was Fred's daughter Margaret (she emigrated) who sent the photograph. Both father and sons were musical; Margaret recalls her father playing the harmonica and an uncle the piano-accordion. The family combined with workers on Baker's threshing machines to form a band and they were known as the *Soot and 'Chine Band* ('Chine being short for machine and pronounced as 'Sheen). Atkins and Atkinson seem to be interchangeable.

50 We have reached Nouns-ley Corner. James Wilkinson (Jimmy), born in 1906, is standing on the right; he was the second son of James senior and his wife Daisy. When his father started a transport and haulage business Jimmy, at the age of 14, could be seen driving a lorry on roads practically devoid of motorised traffic. The original lorries doubled as buses; straw bales lined the insides, serving as seats when taking factory girls to work at Hoffmann's at Chelmsford, or when making trips to the seaside. It was a simple matter to remove the bales in order to carry goods. This particular vehicle looks brand new, and it was perhaps to mark its arrival that the two men are smartly dressed sporting a flower in the buttonhole of the lapels. Late in the afternoon, freshly-picked produce from local farms and from as far away as Tiptree was collected. Rising at 3 a.m., drivers then delivered the loads to Covent Garden in London.

51 As a young boy James junior contracted tuberculosis. When he later broke his leg he was unable to drive and his father set him up as a shopkeeper in the small tin shed. Two wooden planks spanned the ditch to the earlier shop, and the garage roof housing the lorries can be seen behind. Jimmy later married, building the house called Beverley (now Porterhouse) for his bride Gladys and where they expanded the shop. When his health improved he took over the growing haulage business while Gladys ran the shop – a very useful asset in this remote part of the village. It stocked everything: groceries, tobacco, soap, soft drinks and stockings. At one time Gladys sold home-made ice cream. Cheese was cut with a wire, dried fruit arrived packed in solid blocks and sugar had to be shovelled into blue paper bags. To the delight of children, Jean, their daughter, arranged affordable, imaginative displays of sweets in the window. The shop closed in March 1976.

52 In Nounsley Road we approach three pairs of cottages. The nearest, easily defined by their porches and lines of lighter brickwork were built by Mr. Perrin. The first house, Dagmar, was rented by the Olivers, their neighbours being the Baker family. The four remaining comprise Berewood Terrace, the middle two, home to the Butchers and Digbys, the last two housing the Poultons and Turnages. Mr. Fred Poulton charged accumulator batteries for wireless sets, his wife Mary returning them by bicycle. In the distance are the six Butlers Cottages, specifically built at right angles to the road to give the inhabitants a view across the fields to the hills beyond. From the road end lived the families of Gilder, Sparkes, Newman, Pring, Taylor and Powell. Marion Ottley recalls helping Miss Newman from No. 3 board the bus to Chelmsford with lots of Pekinese dogs on leads. She then took the train to exhibit them at Crufts.

NOUNSLEY HATFIELD PEVEREL

53   Deeds of Nounsley Villa show it to date back to before 1772, when it is mentioned as: *a cottage with field or parcel of land, approximately one acre and barn,* given by John Ellis to his youngest son Robert. It probably stayed much the same for many years, one of its owners, Mrs. Emily Chappelow, being remembered as a suffragette. Many people still recall it as the home of Mr. and Mrs. Peter Smith, a kindly couple. To the left and behind was a large orchard and Mr. Smith would lay out ripe fruit on the privet hedge, which then bordered the road, for the local children to eat. Mr. David Hawes, who was born in one of the many bedrooms of his grandfather's house, tells of the dairy built within the house at the back, and below floor level. The white-painted shed on the right was both stable and workshop: a wooden stool cost 6d. Tall elms once stood on what is now Priory Farm Estate and the orchard covered from Priory Close down to Villa Orchard.

54   Curled contentedly on the hedge inside the gate sits the white cat. Beyond Nounsley Villa this gate was the entrance to a row of Mr. Ratcliff's cottages, while a path running along behind the houses served all six. In the gap between the two blocks of dwellings, and scarcely visible, was the communal wash-house in front of which stood a well. Remembered by his daughter as living at number one, far left, was Cyril Silas Hills Spooner (nicknamed 'Dodd'), a well-known and colourful character. Often seen walking his little Jack Russell terrier, 'Dodd' worked as a stockman. Next door lived the Oliver family with the Binks as neighbours. Beyond the gap lived Mr. and Mrs. Dow, then the Seymours and lastly the Hodges family. This last house was bigger, having two rooms upstairs and two down, compared with the other five which were of the 'one up, one down' variety. Well might the cat be content for, in general, the families lived in close harmony.

55 On 2nd September 1914, less than a month into the Great War, the photographer disturbed these two small boys in their make-believe sword fight. Known as Barnards and Gates, the farmhouse has stood at the junction of Nounsley Road and Sportsman's Lane for around five hundred years; on the map it has been corrected from the wrongly-named 'Red Robins', a house nearby. In 1921 the property, and much of the surrounding area, was owned by Mr. Edgar Barralet of Middlefield, in Ulting Road, and occupied by one of his employees, Mr. 'Chabber' Braybrooke. The large walnut tree dropped its nuts in due season and those that fell into the road were free to all. Mr. Eric Ottley recalls the orchard behind the farm where chickens ran free, and the unusual gift that Mr. Braybrooke possessed: he could 'smell' a rabbit, would pause in his steps, and pull one out from the grass beside his feet. The post box built into the brick wall was not removed until the early 1960s.

56 This tiny patch of a green is situated on the corner by Gates Farmhouse. In the 1920s the Salvation Army would march here every Sunday to play. The house facing us is Rose Cottage, which had a beehive in the garden, and at different times was the home of the Baker family and of Billy Gatford. The road on the left slopes down to the ford while the dip behind the grassy slope (now with houses) was once the site of a sawpit for the Priory Estate. Gravel had been extracted by Mr. Wilkinson. In summer time, Albert Valentine recalls that the air above the pit was thronged with sand-martins and the exposed banks were peppered with their nest holes. He reminisces on the plight of three boys: the two Cook brothers and Tom Lapwood (upper Nounsley gang) shut up for a day in a tin hut that stood at the bottom of the pit. They had been locked in by lower Nounsley gang: Albert, his brothers, the Oliver boys, and Tom and Alan Hills!

57　These cottages lie between Priory Farm and the Sportsman's Arms. In the nearest of the three lived Percy and Rose Valentine, next door the Atkinsons, and lastly the Hunwicks. Albert Valentine, eldest of three boys, describes the cottages as being typically 'two rooms up and two rooms down'. Light downstairs was shed by a paraffin lamp, and a candle in a jam jar lit the children up to bed. Coal was stored in a cupboard underneath the stairs. The lavatory was at the bottom of the garden and a communal wash-house, used on a rota system, stood alongside. Water came from a well. They kept chickens; plum, pear and damson trees provided fruit and watercress was gathered from a ditch of running water close to the house. When Mr. Baker's threshing machine was in use at nearby Priory Farm stackyard they killed the mice that ran out. Their father died when the boys were very young, his widow receiving a pension of 21 shillings a week.

58 A merry band of men assemble outside the Sportsman's Arms in readiness for an outing to Clacton. Judging from the crates and jars of alcohol displayed, the mood on the return journey will be even merrier! Far left, trousers supported by braces, and with one of his small daughters by his side, stands the landlord, Mr. H. Rowe. In marked contrast, the suitably and smartly uniformed driver rests one hand on the steering wheel. The vehicle was originally produced as a three-ton lorry for the War Department; between 1916 and 1921 some 12,000 were built. Hostilities over, our revellers' vehicle: Reg HK 8948, Type DEC. 45 HP. was bought up by the National Omnibus & Transport Company and registered on 4th June 1920. At their Moulsham works in Chelmsford it was converted into a charabanc and the document states: *For use as a public conveyance*. It certainly conveyed many of the public here. No doubt a good time was had by all.

59 The frame of horse chestnut leaves outside the Sportsman's exactly pinpoints this location. Uniformed firemen pose beside the car – note the ladders on the roof. No local fire brigade records exist before 1916 when the horse-drawn crew from Witham, two miles distant, attended. In 1939 a local team of occasional firemen was formed of which Mr. W. Cheek, seen here third from the right, was one. Two maroons were set off by Mr. E.G. Claydon, who then drove in his car to collect the men; equipment comprised a small pump and truck. The house in the background is called Whitegates. It was built in the early 1400s, and a listed building report mentions a rare feature. We read: … *the roof is mainly original, with heavily smoke-blackened rafters … and laths and thatch … proving that the lower thatch has been undisturbed since the 1500s …* In 1920 it was bought by Louis Cleave as three cottages, occupied by Perkin, Lester and Algar.

60 This view of houses on the left, seen on a hot summer's day, condenses three into one. Named Clere Cottage, Lightfoots, and Hillcrest they form part of a once closely-knit group of families at Nounsley Green. In the first, once lived the Olds, and Mrs. Old is remembered as acting as midwife at the birth of all the Rowe children at the nearby Sportsman's Arms. The central house was home to the Tanners, where daughter Lil kept many cats. Almost out of sight lies the third house, where Charles and Clara Gilder, parents to fourteen children, lived. Charles, a fishmonger, went his rounds selling the fish. One daughter, Emily, went into service in Yorkshire at the age of 10, later marrying Harry Hills from Sussex. Tom and Alan, local residents, are their sons. In the house opposite lived the Turnages, grandparents to Mrs. Hills, and at one time they kept the pub; Mr. Robert Turnage is listed in 1862 as *beer retailer at Nounsley Green.*

61 Once two cottages with a central chimney stack, this unusual house was set back in the shrubby area on the left of Robert Turnage's home (opposite). In it lived Mr. and Mrs. William Steele, senior, a butcher, who had eleven children, some of them seen here. It was built of tar-covered wood and had two entrances and two staircases: one at the front and one at the back. In the garden they kept chickens and pigs. Margaret Wagstaff, daughter of Olive Steele (tall and in a white blouse), remembers that when the men were tarring the left side of the house she climbed their ladder to the tiny window, and looking down saw all her aunts in their white aprons looking up, apprehensive in case she should fall. She also recalls tarring over her grandmother's front door step! After buying beasts at Chelmsford market, grandfather, who enjoyed a small bet on the horses, took refreshment at the Railway Tavern – his horse and cart finding its own way home.

62 This elegant portrait is of one of the Old family. The following item came from a newspaper dated 20th November 1891. *LOST AND FOUND. The village was all agog on Saturday when it became known that two boys, George and Charles, sons of Mr. Seaborn Old, gamekeeper to Rev. C.G. Townsend of Berwick Place, had gone astray. It appears that these promising youths aged about 14 and 10 respectively, had lost a ferret, belonging to their father, and unless they found it they were promised 'no breakfast' on Saturday morning. They decided to run away with the intention of walking to London where an aunt of theirs lives. Having reached* Brentwood they sought help from a Dr. Quennell who sheltered them overnight. On Sunday morning their father proceeded to London to inform the authorities at Scotland Yard of his loss. During his absence Sgt. Allen of Witham received a telegram as to their whereabouts. They were received home with open arms.

63 Bridge Farm, at the foot of Nounsley Hill, has been recorded since 1327 when it belonged to Juliana atte Bregge. It lies close to the ford where the River Ter trickles gently across the road. Do not be deceived. At times of heavy rain the Ter's waters swirl ever-wider, spreading over the flat ground; Mr. Eric Ottley recalls stepping through the door on the left – straight into water. Mrs. Madeleine Sorrell tells of the house being cut off to the south by the water, the family having to leave by the back door and climb the field sloping up to Sportsman's Lane. She also recalls that her father, 'Dodd' Spooner, having thatched a barn at the farm returned to discover that the children had used it as a slide and he had the work to do again. He was not best pleased! Families recalled as living here bear the names of Carrington, Vincent and Taylor. In a recent flood a car, trapped in the water, was carried along the river.

64 Leaving Bridge Farm behind us we splash through the ford or cross the narrow railed bridge to proceed up the hill to make our way along Mowden Hall Lane. This small wooden boarded cottage once stood adjacent to the house named Mowden Hall Cottage – quite unmistakable, for it bears on the gate a plaque which reads: *Never Mind the Dog, Beware of the Owner.* Next to the house is a small pond. In this wooden cottage, probably converted from a stable, lived Arthur and Charlotte Butcher and their family. Arthur was a stockman and gardener at Mowden Hall Farm. Their home was cosy: a living room, two bedrooms and a kitchen that stretched the length of the cottage. Here Rhoda Butcher and her mother are pictured in the front garden among the flowers. Rhoda remembers riding in the cake-cart and helping her father to grind cake for the cows. As Arthur sat hand-milking the cows he was surrounded by the farm cats hoping to catch any stray squirts.

65 The origins of Mowden Hall (spelt in many ways) date back a known eight hundred years. The photograph we see here by Spalding, is of the back of the house and includes the moat. It is not the original building. Confusingly, the house now has another name while a modern Mowden Hall stands next to Mowden Hall Cottage. Rhoda Butcher's father was a worker here for 56 years. In the 1920s, when the occupants were Mr. and Mrs. Doyne, Lily Butcher, wife of Rhoda's brother Jack, worked in the house as cook. Rhoda played with the children of the Doyne family and recalls that the servants' bedrooms were at the top of the house and that the grounds sloped all the way down to World's End and the river. One day she and Peggy Doyne climbed on to the roof of a pig sty which gave way, depositing them among the pigs! In the pea-picking season, travellers lived in a bothy (outhouse), cooked on a stove, and slept in mangers on straw palliasses in one of the cowsheds.

MOWDEN HALL. 494.

66   Rainbirds, or Chelmer Farm is the last house in the village before crossing the river into Little Baddow. The house is partly sixteenth-century, the east end has wooden carvings, and the central chimney stack is of interest. It was once two cottages and some doors and windows have been repositioned. Mr. and Mrs. Smith moved from the left-hand part when the Joslin family moved out from the larger section on the right. Sitting downstairs one night Mrs. Smith heard a terrified scream from above. One of the children had woken to see a soldier standing at the foot of the bed. At a later date the family discovered that one of the Joslin family, a soldier serving abroad in the Second World War, had been killed on that day. When flood waters lap the front doorstep the river has covered around 130 yards and risen six feet. The present owners recall the bravery of Mr. Eddie Webb who rescued a lady driver from her car, swept along in torrential rain.

67 On now to Ulting. All Saints' School, seen here on the right with its porch, was built in 1865. An 1890 directory states that it was built to take sixty children, average attendance was 35 and Miss Hinton was the mistress. At one time or another the 21 Grout children from Stock Hall (of whom later) attended the school swelling the numbers. Mr. and Mrs. George Bowles lived in part of the School House, seen next door, occupying only the rooms at the rear, while Miss Hinton lived in the two rooms at the front. George's children had no difficulty in arriving at school on time having but a few steps to walk. Percy, was the name of one of his boys.

By 1917 the school had closed, the pupils then going to Woodham Walter, Hatfield Peverel or Langford to receive their education. They would have walked or, if lucky, had a ride on a waggon. Miss Hinton had moved to Hatfield Peverel where she taught Renee Ashby, Percy's future bride-to-be.

68 Mr. George Bowles poses a little self-consciously beside his front door. He has moved from his former home to buy the bungalow on the other side of the school and has become sub-postmaster of Ulting. Letters came through Maldon arriving at 8.10 a.m. and were despatched at 4.15 p.m. Entry to the office was through the front door where, inside to the right, was a little hatch beside which hung a small bell. On hearing the sound, Lizzie, George's wife, would lift the hatch and go to the requisite drawer for stamps or postal orders. The letter box can be seen on the outside wall beneath the post office sign. Leaning nonchalantly on his bicycle is the postman, Mr. Gower, who cycled from Maldon each morning. Once at Ulting he carried out his delivery over a very wide area before cycling back in the early evening. George, for long-service of over sixty years, was awarded a medal. 'They were a dear old couple' says Mrs. Renee Bowles.

69 An abrupt left turn beyond the former post office leads down a narrow track. At the end stands the Ulting parish church of All Saints in what must surely be regarded as one of the most delightful of positions. Very small, early English in style, and made from stone and flint, it has a wooden turret with a shingled spire commensurate with its proportions. It borders the River Chelmer. George Bowles was a busy man for he served 68 years as churchwarden, during which time he stood as godfather to more babies than he could remember. In so sparsely populated a parish too few people were available to act in that capacity. During all his time here, the river, when in spate, brimmed the bottom of the south door but never flooded inside. Today the tiny, still-hallowed churchyard, is a stopping point for pleasure barges and a quiet spot for reflection.

The cottages (now one) in the background formerly housed three families.

70   At Hoe Mill the River Chelmer marks the boundary between Ulting and Woodham Walter. In Hervey Benham's book *Some Essex Water Mills* he states that the illustration in chapter 9 is the only ' surviving picture of the Mill which stands in Woodham Walter. The one shown here is from a slightly different angle and the photographer is unknown. Benham writes (in 1976) that: ... *Signposts still pointed to the mills ... although there have been no mills to point to for over 60 years ... so this scene too, must have been taken before 1916. In a Quarter Sessions Roll of 1626, Matthew Pease is ordered ... to scour ditches and lop trees between Ho Mill gate on the highway towards Maldon. The Mill* once had its own horse-drawn barges named the *Hopewell* and the *Seven Sisters*. Today small sailing craft are moored on the Ulting side beyond the Lock House, while the pleasure boat *Victoria* plies a pleasant course from the Paper Mills close to Chelmer Farm.

Hoe Mill.

71 Mrs. Wendy Russell's father, Ernie Grant, was once lock keeper at Hoe Mill, the family living in the house on the right. He, like so many lock-keepers before him, was responsible for the opening and closing of the gates and for this stretch of river. It was near here that Mr. Bowen-Davies kept his sheep as did a farmer on the other side. Some fell into the river where their thick fleece, saturated with water, meant they drowned. Bargees on spotting them would fish out the carcasses flinging them on alternate occasions to either side of the bank. Mr. Cant sometimes had a more macabre duty to perform. If a body was found floating in the river, he would phone Hatfield Peverel Police Station; this at a time when constables were not only resident in the village but covered the area on pedal cycles. Should the body be on the far bank, P.C. Ted Arthy, a greatly respected, and down-to-earth man, would laconically remark: 'Then you'd better ring Danbury'!

LOCK & LOCK HOUSE. NEAR ULTING

72 Ulting Wick Farm, home for many years to Gerwyn Bowen-Davies and his family, stands between the school and Hoe Mill. Although some distance from the river, at times of flood the sight of swans sailing across the front lawn meant the waters had risen! Farming was mixed, covering some 200 acres. They kept cows and horses (all known by name) and by the river there were sheep; the remaining land was arable. An interesting Tillage Journal, kept between 1912 and 1915 by Gerwyn's sister, shows a map of the farm and an account of crops grown. Peas included Harrison's Glory, Essex Stars, and Earliest of All. Cereal varieties were: Black Tartar Oats, Wilhelmina Wheat and Square-Headed Master. Mangels listed were Garton's Long Red and Webb's Golden Lion. Mr. Bowen-Davies also grew barley, kohl-rabi, potatoes, clover (red and white) beans, tares and turnips. Sadly, having survived the 1920's Depression the farm was sold at a loss in 1936.

ULTING WICK

73 Off now to Doe's Corner. The saying: *from small acorns mighty oak trees grow* is certainly true of the Doe family, for 1998 sees the year of their centenary celebration. In this photograph of 1899, Ernest Doe, the proprietor, is the dominant figure standing before the new, purpose-built forge proudly advertising *E. Doe, General Smith and Implement Agent*. Three workmen stand behind. On 2nd March 1893, Ernest was apprenticed by his father, Charles Doe, miller of Terling, to serve with George Wood, blacksmith of Hatfield Peverel. Among conditions imposed on Ernest were: *He shall not contract matrimony within the said Term, not play at Cards or Dice Tables or any other unlawful Games … haunt Taverns or Playhouses*. The apprenticeship was successfully completed and in September 1898, on George's retirement, Charles Doe bought the firm for his son. Today four successive generations have run what is now a nationally-known business.

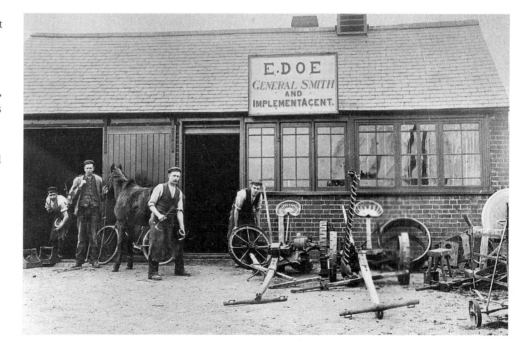

74   Romance links this and the next card. Thomas Cullen of The Elms, popular farmer and member of the Witham firm of seed merchants, lived here from 1919 to 1939. Farming was mixed arable, and they had six horses, one milking cow, pigs and store cattle. Tom fell in love with Violet Grout (looking after ageing parents) from the adjacent farm of Stock Hall. Knowing that Violet's parents would resent the marriage each secretly left home one morning, and Tom, aged 46, and Violet, 34, tied the knot at Maldon Registry Office at 8.30 a.m. Violet's mother threw a fit but her father commented: *There's a bottle of champagne in the cupboard.*

Thomas told his father who arranged delivery, by horse and cart, of a brass bedstead. With all this drama, it is perhaps not surprising that their eldest child of three (Anne, Walter and Margaret), took up acting. For thirty years Anne played the part on radio of Carol Gray (Grenville/Tregorran) in *The Archers*.

75   At the end of a lane beyond Doe's Corner and The Elms is Stock Hall Farm. Here lived Walter and Sophia Grout with their exceptionally large family – 21 children. Fourth youngest was Violet; fortunately the house was large, for 15 to 20 sat down to Sunday lunch. Sophia had married at 18 and after the birth of each child the family doctor would bring her a keg of oysters and send her to the seaside for a holiday. The little Grouts attended Ulting school. At 12 Violet made bread for all the family; later her mother sent her to Bourne & Hollingsworth in London to learn the 'rag-trade', paying one shilling a week for her apprenticeship and keep. In the First World War she joined the V.A.D. returning after to care for her parents. Three brothers lived to their 90s, two sisters to be 101 and 102, but sadly her own husband Tom died in 1939. In 1997, shortly after taking part in a television discussion, this grand old lady, Violet Cullen, died, aged 108.

76   It is here at Langford church that we will bring our tour to a close. William Oliver, baker from Hatfield Peverel, delivered bread to this small village, and it was at Wickham Bishops and Langford that trains stopped on the branch line from Witham to Maldon. The many Grout children, attired in their Sunday best, regularly attended religious instruction at the church and, when old enough, joined their parents in the family pew. Almost unbelievably, in such a large family, only two children died young: one drowned in a pond, the other from lockjaw after a cut arm had been bound with a cobweb by a well-intentioned aunt. Here they lie buried. Here too, at peace, lie the parents of a prodigious family, Walter and Sophia Grout. Both died of old age and on exactly the same day. In this tranquil spot we will take our leave of them; they, having reached the end of life's journey, and we, our journey through Hatfield Peverel and Ulting.

Langford Village. Maldon.